MW01092821

Union Proof

CREATING YOUR SUCCESSFUL
UNION FREE STRATEGY

Peter J. Bergeron

First published by Dog Ear Publishing
4010 W. 86th Street, Ste H
Indianapolis, IN 46268
www.dogearpublishing.net

ISBN: 978-159858-747-0

This book is printed on acid-free paper.

Printed in the United States of America

Please Note:

These materials have been prepared by Projections for informational purposes only and are not legal advice. Transmission of the information is not intended to create, and receipt does not constitute, a client relationship. Projections is not a persuader as defined by the NLMRDA, nor do we employ any consultants or attorneys. Internet users should not act upon this information without seeking professional counsel. The information contained in this document is provided only as general information that may or may not reflect the most current legal developments. This information is not intended to constitute legal advice or to substitute for obtaining legal advice from an attorney licensed in your state or country. This document may be considered advertising under applicable state laws and ethical rules.

The document you now hold in your hands represents an enormous amount of knowledge on both labor relations and employee communications. Projections has been helping companies – from the largest in the world to those you've never even heard of – maintain positive relationships with their employees for 30 years. We take pride in the resources we offer, and the success our clients have enjoyed over the years has helped us refine, improve and perfect those resources.

After 33 years with General Dynamics, primarily in Human Resources, Peter Bergeron is now focusing on helping Projections assist other companies in creating positive employee relationships and maintaining union-free environments. In his time at General Dynamics, Peter utilized the employee communication resources offered by Projections numerous times, and is now working to bring the success he found through those tools to other companies. I personally worked with Peter on the Quonset Point Electric Boat campaigns. Peter was instrumental in helping Projections perfect the use of custom video working in tandem with custom websites during a pre-election campaign, to communicate with Electric Boat families as well as employees.

Peter's knowledge and experience are vast, and we have decided to compile a small amount of that knowledge here for the use of our friends and colleagues. We hope that you will find Peter's insight valuable in your own efforts to maintain positive employee relationships without the need for a third party.

If you have any questions regarding the use or application of any of the labor relations or employee communication products referenced in this document, please don't hesitate to contact me directly.

Walter Orechwa
CEO, Projections, Inc.
waltero@projectionsinc.com
877-448-9741

Peter's Story

As you read through this document, you'll begin to understand that there is no magic wand when it comes to remaining union-free. It's an ongoing process that requires constant communication and vigilance. When upper management makes a conscious decision and says, "We need to make an effort to be union-free," terrific. But that's a strategic decision that needs to involve multiple players and a great deal of thought and effort.

Unfortunately many companies choose to do nothing. This leaves them vulnerable to unionizing efforts. Many are faced with the scenario where they are caught unaware by an organizing drive, or worse yet, by a petition for election.

We'll deal with both of these situations in the pages to follow. I'll also provide information on some of the best ways to remain union-free.

For the purposes of keeping us both in the same frame of mind, every company fits into one of the following four phases of unionization, which are very often cyclical in nature:

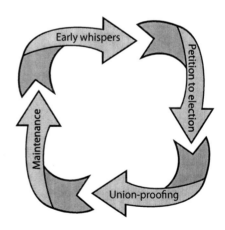

1. Union-Free maintenance

2. Early whispers (pre-petition)

3. Petition phase to election

4. Post-election union-proofing

There's no set time table that any of the phases follow – quite literally, companies can happily spend years in the union-free maintenance phase, without even being consciously aware that that's what they're doing.

But without a strategic plan in place to keep them union free, companies often find themselves in the midst of a full-blown union campaign and wonder how it happened.

The Real Cost of Unionization

Often, companies in the early stages of developing their union-free strategy want to know what's at stake – what are the human costs, the opportunity costs, and the monetary costs they could face as a result of unionization. The answer here is different for every company because there are a variety of factors that can come into play, such as:

- Size and location of the company
- Culture, including flexibility
- Communication philosophy
- Corporate and Supervisory Structure
- Industry
- Business Community Relationships

...and many other varying factors. But the answer to the basic question of the cost of unionization can best be derived from looking at companies who have both unionized and union-free business units, as we would expect the above factors to be constant, regardless of union status. In these situations, it is generally accepted that administrative costs are 25-35% higher in the unionized facilities. Those hard costs can come from:

- Personnel time spent on Collective Bargaining, Strike Contingency Planning, and Strikes
- Additional Human Resources staff
- Personnel time spent with government agencies
- Labor Consultants and Attorneys
- Additional labor costs due to rules on overtime, administration, grievances and arbitration processing, union steward time off the job

Employees can also experience the divisiveness a union can bring – when co-workers disagree on union issues, long-term friendships often suffer. Additional on-the-job stress can occur if employees do not take pride in their work, mistrust management, or if customers see a drop in quality or service. Employees will pay dues, and can become disillusioned when they don't feel the union is accomplishing what employees thought they would, or that bargaining is simply not progressing quickly enough.

And in many cases, the cost of unionization extends beyond the walls of the company. Restrictive union rules can predetermine promotions and work assignments, overtime schedules and other factors that can cause stress that carries over into home life. Beyond that, employees and their families can experience the financial difficulties of a strike, historically creating stress on marriages, parenthood, and other important relationships.

What I Learned About Maintaining Positive Relations

Years of working with a staff of top-notch employee relations experts, consultants, attorneys, and even line employees who felt such pride in their work that they came forward to assist in the fight against unionization, brought me to some basic but significant conclusions. The great news here is that it is possible to avoid unionization by enacting a proactive strategy and having a plan in place if an organizing drive begins or a petition for election is filed.

UNION FREE
"Union-proofing" Acronym

U - understand any organizing attempt is real
N - never wait - have your union avoidance plan in place
I - identify the real and perceived issues
O - openly communicate - early, often & aggressively
N - know the numbers - 30%, 50% + 1, union dues $, etc.

F - get the family involved immediately
R - respect the rights of employees and the union
E - educate all employees involved
E - energize first line supervisors

When I reflect back on why I was so successful in helping some General Dynamics business units avoid unionization, I think it was very simple. When I spoke to supervisors about the perils of working in a unionized environment I spoke with conviction and a passion of what a union can do to a business. I would tell them that even if they had an axe to grind with the management of their facility (and they thought that a union would be a good way of paying the company back), they were sadly mistaken - they would only be making a bad situation worse, and their job would become a nightmare. I would try to rally supervisors to positively communicate to their employees the real facts about belonging to a union.

I grew up the son of a shipyard worker. I knew my dad was both a very conscientious worker and proud of the product that he built. He was a welder and an inspector of nuclear submarines and worked at the shipyard just shy of 40 years. Unfortunately, some of my childhood and teenage memories are of the bitter arguments and family struggles that occurred when the union that represented the hourly shipyard workers went on strike. These strikes sometimes lasted a few weeks to several months. While my dad at times contemplated crossing the picket line to support our family, he also knew that this decision was a career-ender. He had witnessed the never-ending torment that union members imposed on others that had crossed the line in previous strikes.

When I graduated from college in 1973, my dad's advice to me was clear and simple: don't go to work for a big unionized company. His rationale was summed up with the opinion that "you are just a number to the company, they don't care about the people, it's production first and nothing else matters." Well, jobs were very scarce in 1973 and I was working as a waiter and bartender and had difficulty finding a job elsewhere. Finally, a buddy of mine got a job at General Dynamic's Electric Boat division and called me and told me to "fill out an application; they are looking for someone like you. " I did exactly what my friend had instructed me to do and totally disregarded my father's advice. I was hired within two weeks. What I didn't know then was that I was hired as a salaried "administrative assistant," replacing a couple of striking clerks from the union that represented the design, technical and clerical employees. My first day on the job, I came to work wearing a brand-new sports jacket, that cost $140 - a lot of money in 1973. I had to squeeze through a picket line, just to get into my new office. When I got to the office, a co-worker of mine asked me, what happened to my nice jacket, as it looked "shiny." I discovered that the picketers had put Vaseline on their raincoats, which rubbed off on the clothing of the folks that tried to get through the picket line. I was absolutely livid when I discovered what had happened - my new sport coat was ruined and there wasn't a thing I could do about it. This was my first bitter taste of union tactics.

I worked five years in production at Electric Boat, and watched first-hand what union stewards got away with. How they vehemently represented employees that should have been fired many times over. How they instructed the folks they represented to "slow down" on the job. I heard them talk about rigging the union elections. I heard them scheme, time and again, how to "make the company pay" for the perceived injustices. I saw the aftermath from union members that beat up employees who were "economic replacements" during a lengthy strike in 1975. Worse yet, I watched an entire shipyard grieve over the unfortunate death of a near-retirement employee. The employee and a union steward had bitterly argued about "super seniority" over a period of weeks, until one day, the arguing became physical and the older employee died – this was a tragic and profound illustration of life in a union environment. I realized early and throughout my career that there had to be a better way.

Five years into my career, I moved into Human Resources and became a Labor Representative. I and another representative handled grievances, arbitrations and discipline for 5,600 employees who were represented by the Boilermakers union. All I did in my first six months on the job was administer discipline to some very unsavory employees. At times, I did fear for my life as I was constantly given veiled threats when I was firing employees. I also was sent to help another division of General Dynamics as they worked to hire replacement workers during a very bitter strike by the IAM. Within three weeks, we had replaced better than a third of the 300+ strikers - something the union said we could never accomplish. This strike was one of the most violent strikes I ever witnessed. I saw cars that were keyed. I witnessed rock throwing, fires lit, fights, and drunken brawls on paydays that were missed. I was still young and very impressionable, and this assignment was one I will never forget.

Shortly after, I moved to the Quincy Shipbuilding Division of General Dynamics in Quincy, MA. I witnessed the stubbornness of the unions not accepting survivability concessions and regrettably saw this 100+ year-old shipyard close its gates forever in 1985. The unions honestly believed that the shipyard would never close and the company was just bluffing. Just prior to the shipyard closing, I was Manager of Labor Relations. During the shipyard closing process, negotiations commenced. The union, in all its arrogance, came into negotiations wanting wage and benefit increases for their remaining members – I found their demands incredible - but very typical for what unions stood for. Unfortunately, 6,500 employees lost their jobs in the process.

After the Quincy shipyard closed, I took a job in Rhode Island, again working for General Dynamics and for Electric Boat Division but for their non-union facility in Quonset Point, RI. I was brought on to run a union avoidance campaign, something I knew nothing about but was eager to learn. This campaign was among the largest organizing campaigns in the nation at the time. That campaign went on for nearly three years, culminating with the union withdrawing their election petition -without an election- in the aftermath of another long strike by the union in Groton, CT. Working at Quonset Point opened my eyes to working in a non-union environment. Teamwork abounded, employees were delighted to cross-train, and supervisors' authority was rarely challenged. Were there issues? Of course there were, but workers and management got together and came to many successful resolutions. I saw the passion in the eyes of managers (many of whom previously worked in unionized environments) to constantly strive to have harmonious relationships with their employees. Many of these managers knew and witnessed firsthand the drawbacks of a unionized workforce.

Some years later, I was asked to return to Quonset Point to take charge of another union avoidance campaign, against the Steelworkers. This time, the campaign went all the way to a petition and a vote, but we were again successful in communicating our position and remaining union-free. I was appointed the Union Avoidance Specialist for General Dynamics, and found myself traveling the country successfully assisting other business units in remaining union free.

Post-retirement, I knew that I could continue to help other companies in their desire to remain union-free. As Projections was an essential component of union-free strategy at Quonset Point, I knew I would be able to assist like-minded companies by joining their team. With Projections, I've been able to witness other companies who remained union-free through successful communication efforts. Recently, I helped a large aerospace company facing an attempt by the IAM. There, I can proudly say I enjoyed the largest margin of victory I ever saw through to an election. The key to success was establishing effective, fact-based communications with employees regarding union representation. A customized Projections "25th Hour" video and custom website were the key contributing factors in this communications-based victory.

What I've learned is that ultimately, the strategies you put into place will evolve into the driving force behind the company's success. Once developed, comprehensive implementation means that a union-free philosophy is part of the corporate culture. The strategies that will evolve from the information in these pages will be based on experience, refined over years of test and trial, and I can promise you that these are the some of the best principles for any company that wants to remain union-free.

Organizing Drive? Don't Panic.

I'm going to begin with the "Early Whispers" (pre-petition) phase of the unionization cycle. If a company is in tune with its employees, this is the point where panic sometimes sets in. It may be quiet – too quiet, and it's easy to see that something is happening, just under the surface of things. Employees are gathered together in groups during break times, a leaflet is seen here or there... subtle signs can be recognized as the beginning stage of an organizing drive. Strategically, this is the most important phase. You've got to begin by analyzing what's going to work best for the company, based on several factors, the first of which is size. Determine if your company is a:

> SSC (Small Size Company) 1-250 employees
> A one-on-one communication strategy is good, primarily because a smaller number of personal messages can be effective.

> MSC (Mid Size Company) 251-1000 employees
> In this range, your strategy will rely on the strength (or weakness) of the relationships between workers and management, and the ways in which employees are accustomed to receiving information.

> LSC (Large Size Company) 1000+ employees
> Larger companies may not have supervisors who are consistently effective. To reach large groups of employees, the strategy must include several approaches that allow employees to receive the information on their own terms.

This one variable, company size, will help determine the amount, type and quality of the communication you should undertake. In general, the smaller the group of employees, the more personal the communication should be. With larger groups, consistency is paramount- differing messages or the inconsistent manner in

Real Life Campaign Experiences
"There were no traditional signs of Union organizing activity - no flyers, no leafleting, no cards in the work areas etc., and, accordingly, management was caught totally by surprise when the petition hit."

which messages are delivered can be a serious weakness.

The next thing to consider is the demographic makeup of the workforce. Are the majority long-term employees or are they new hires with relatively little knowledge of the company? Take a close look at age, race, sex, education, language barriers, and employee knowledge levels on unions and on the company. Understanding the impact of these factors will further shape your communications strategy.

Finally, evaluate the information you have complied. The understanding gained at this time should continue to guide communications throughout the campaign, and once you define who your employees are, it's time to answer one of the most important questions: What are the employees' needs? We'll come back to this in Chapter Two, as we address the issues.

Assemble Your Team
Regardless of size, every company that hears early whispers should engage a labor attorney. Additionally, an outside labor relations consultant may be an attorney recommendation for all MSC's and LSC's. With both of these experts, there are differing styles. You can find a "hands-off" attorney and/or consultant, which can be cost-effective. What this type of involvement provides is a safety-net approach. Once you've retained an attorney or consultant, when you are in need of advice or counsel, you simply contact him or her with your (well organized) questions.

At the opposite end of the spectrum, some companies prefer to have full-time attorneys and consultants who will literally "move in" and dedicate themselves to your company's quest

> *"The company engaged an outside legal firm and hired a full time outside consultant familiar with the company and the prior organizing campaigns. A full time staff assistant was brought on board. One vital employee was initially assigned to the campaign for two days per week from September through December and then full time beginning in January 2001. I was brought on board as the campaign chairperson. We quickly launched meetings with the managers on all shifts and started retraining all supervision on the "Do's and Don'ts" involved in a union organizing campaign. We established a "war room" as the command center for all campaign related activities. The above is pretty much the standard operating procedure in any campaign and I wouldn't recommend changing the practice at all."*

to remain union-free. Their full-time attention to your company, your issues, and your employees can be vital to the effectiveness of your strategy, and can be paramount to avoiding the minefield the union has created.

Internally, you need to hand-select the people you think will be the most effective players in executing the strategy you're going to develop. Who understands the employees and truly connects with them? That can be the person who will provide you with insight into the perceived issues. (See Chapter Two for more on the issues.) Who among your staff has experience in Labor Relations? That person can help you identify pockets of vulnerability. (See Chapter Three for more on gauging vulnerability.)

Rules of Engagement
Once your team is assembled, define the ways in which you will operate. Designate a central location for meetings, and discuss how and when you will communicate with one another. Due to the simple "nature of the beast, " many of these factors will be defined in a reactionary way, but if you begin establishing control from the beginning, the entire team will feel empowered to move forward with the strategy you develop.

Determine early on what method of communicating with your employees and their families will work best for your business. There is no proven method that works for every business. Many times the business culture will drive the communication vehicles. Review and decide upon internal/external communication methods e.g. "All Team Notices", team meetings conducted by supervisors, custom videos for hourly and/or management, home mailings from the site managers/president, custom union-free websites, etc.

Identify the Issues

As the campaign evolves, regardless of whether a petition is filed resulting in a vote, you need to be on the lookout for what got the company there in the first place. To understand that path, you need to identify the issues – what's driving the campaign? Are these issues part of a larger "iceberg" you can't see? What's not immediately obvious? Often, it's not the most overt problems – it's the more subtle things-the individual needs-that lead employees to a union. So often I hear the phrase- "it is the little things we didn't do that got us to this point."

Take advantage of the strength of the team you have assembled, because they are readily available with a wealth of information that can be helpful to you. Ask them to assist you in determining what factors led employees to consider joining a union. Place a concentrated effort into defining any perceived slights or injustices, as well as problems or issues that could not be resolved in the past.

Now, evaluate the strength of your current leadership. First, closely assess your supervisors – how well do they communicate, how knowledgeable are they? How connected are they with their employees? Even if you have the best supervisors who have outstanding communication skills, you may still need labor relations training at the supervisory level if they are unfamiliar with organizing drives, ULPs, and union tactics.

> *"From the petition date forward, the site manager formally took on a lead role, which was extremely beneficial. This resulted in unifying his staff to work through any and all issues during the final weeks of the campaign. During those weeks, there were significant amounts of quality communication and positive teamwork, which bought the entire group closer together towards the common goal of remaining union-free."*

Next, look higher – are there any unpopular leaders above front line supervisors or even at the corporate level? While communication is paramount at this time, some executives may be better seen than heard. With other key executives, you will need to impress upon them the importance of remaining open, available, and hyper-aware during this crucial period. Remember: issues are sometimes so subtle they may seem insignificant, but nothing could be further from the truth.

As the old adage goes, "perception is reality," but now is the time to uncover misconceptions, half-truths and any other minefields the union may have planted in the minds of your employees. In their enthusiasm for organizing, is the union possibly missing the true issues? What's a real issue vs. what the union has "created?" Anything that provides you an opening to address real issues can damage the union's credibility and strengthen your position.

Your team's job is to help identify the issues of the campaign. This intelligence can be invaluable if used properly to factually and consistently address those items that are truly of concern to a majority of the employees. For example, in one campaign I was involved in, discussions led us to the realization that many employees were disillusioned with regard to growth and promotion. Apparently they were told by one of the HR managers during the hiring process that they could expect to be rewarded for their hard work and dedication within weeks after being hired, but this just simply was not true.

Other issues I've seen involved employees that felt too much emphasis was placed on the production side of the business, resulting in a lack of attention to individual employees. I watched misunderstandings about an existing seniority system turn into fear that older workers would be laid off. Rumors about the strength of the union can become an issue. Bitterness from things that happened many years ago can be harbored with long-term workers. Whatever the issues are, root them out and bring them to the forefront of your union avoidance campaign. Make sure your communication strategy makes room to address each issue.

As you are able to identify the issues more clearly, create short-term communications pieces and have them available and ready to

> *"We felt the need to continue the union avoidance/awareness education process with not only the hourly, but more importantly with our front line supervision. Most campaigns are won or lost via the impact of the first line supervisors. Accordingly, we began several weeks of informational sessions and labor relations training with supervisors on all three shifts. We also provided wage and benefit comparisons. This effort diffused a number of wage and benefit issues that existed due to misinformation and also rumors that were fueled by a competitor's strike settlement agreement."*

distribute. Anything that quickly and easily provides clarity on a volatile issue can be the foundation for additional in-depth communication later on. After the team has been assembled, it may become apparent that the company has a very small window of opportunity to get out ahead of the union's momentum. If so, move very quickly and begin to educate both the management team and the hourly employees about the facts involved in signing union authorization cards or a union petition. Once this action is taken, you may see positive feedback from employees who support your union-free philosophy, and who are often pleased to see that the company cares enough to go on the offensive. This immediate effort will also show union sympathizers that you're serious about your union avoidance campaign and position on remaining union-free.

Finally, don't dismiss any issues that were created by the union without analyzing them. Organizers have historically preyed on the underlying fear of employees that they could be laid off or fired at any moment. While the union's claim of "protection" from "at-will" employment may be hollow and unnecessary, if employees buy into it their fear can become a powerful weapon for the union.

Pockets of Vulnerability

If you're thinking proactively, I'm willing to bet you may already know where you're most vulnerable. You may have even hired a consultant or survey firm to conduct a vulnerability assessment. But if you've found yourself in the midst of an organizing drive, you may not have had the time to do these things. If that's the case, it's time to conduct your own analysis of the situation and identify pockets of vulnerability.

Assemble your team once again and take a look at the information you have. Those on your team with labor relations experience will be most in tune with what's going on, the strategies and tactics the union is using, and how your employees are reacting to them. Then, ask the questions, "What are our strengths?" and, "Where do our weaknesses lie?"

> "Collectively, we decided to challenge the union's inclusion of all employees with the title of Captain. We felt that there was sufficient evidence that their job responsibilities were clearly supervisory and thereby excluded under the NLRA."

The answers may be in compensation, policies, individual managers or supervisors, or even in the underlying attitude of the team itself. Flexibility is a huge strength that you can capitalize on, especially if employees enjoy job flexibility, versatility in training opportunities, and a culture that encourages and implements employee suggestions.

Conversely, one of the worst weaknesses to have is the belief that you already know how to avoid unionization. Be gut-wrenchingly honest when determining your strengths and weaknesses. Remember that every situation, every employee, every company, and every union is different. NEVER underestimate the capacity of the union to surprise management.

Once you "really feel you know the union," stop. Pinch yourself and wake up! You are on the verge of a dangerous "union avoidance no-no" - complacency.

Take a careful look at how the campaign is evolving in order to identify any vulnerability directly related to how the campaign is being run. If you've reached the point where the union has filed a petition for election, examine that peition closely for areas of weakness. Who is the bargaining unit as defined by the union's petition? Do you want to make any changes to their definition? You'll need to make strategic decisions before going to the NLRB and agreeing to the stipulations that will define the makeup of the unit. Your attorney can be very valuable in this area. Remember: historically, larger bargaining units are more difficult to organize. As risky as it may sound, it might be strategically advantageous to add on additional areas and employees to your unit definition if you feel they are predominantly pro-company.

As the campaign begins to solidify, be sure you're looking as closely at how the union is running their campaign as you are at your own strategies. Is their approach traditional, with flyers, meetings, etc. or more unconventional with seemingly shifting strategies, barely perceptible communication and no serious timeline? Some campaigns (and some unions) are nearly impossible to figure out, and while the organizers may be intentionally keeping you guessing, it's also possible that their strategy is lacking. No matter what you are able to readily observe, realize that their campaign can become stronger than you know. I'll never forget seeing the Teamsters' "Welcome Wagon" (a giant tractor trailer with the Teamsters logos on it) parked outside our company one morning after weeks of no overt activity.

The next step is to conduct a straw poll. Assemble your supervisors and ask them to tell you if the vote were today, how would your employees vote? Each supervisor should specifically look at each employee and decide as to how they think those employees would vote. There will always be some misconceptions or errors in judgment, but, in my experience, conducting these polls multiple times leading up to an election will provide a fairly accurate assessment of the outcome. Conducting multiple straw polls also sheds light on any migration of employee sentiment.

In order for these straw polls to truly help you define your vulnerable points without putting you at risk for ULPs or a contested election, you'll need to train your supervisors in how to gauge employee affiliations. This means specific labor relations training, crafted for the sole purpose of keeping you union-free. This training should include information on union history and how unionization can affect a company, as well as general good communication training that will help your supervisors better connect with employees. It should also cover authorization cards, specific tactics the union may take, and should teach supervisors how to talk to employees about the things the union may be saying or doing.

Realize that you need to continue the union avoidance/awareness education process with both hourly employees and front line supervision through the course of the campaign (and even beyond, if you want to avoid future organizing drives). If you must focus on one group, however, focus on your supervisors. As mentioned earlier, most campaigns are won or lost via the impact of the first line supervisors.

Next, see if the union itself is a point of vulnerability for you. What kind of track record do they have

> *"We immediately conducted a straw poll of all full-time and part-time employees and the results were strongly in support of the union."*

at the local level? At the international level? Are they using smaller victories to try and convince workers of their strength? Realize that these things can become larger than life to employees who think they need union protection. If the union is touting their own successes, your best strategy is to do your homework and communicate all the facts about the union.

If the union is working the angle of strength in numbers, for example, find out how much reality there is behind their claims. Compare their membership statistics locally, regionally and nationally. Assess their strength in your industry as well, and find factual comparisons that limit your vulnerability.

All of this research can be used in communications with employees, and I successfully worked with Projections in crafting a number of custom video presentations and union free web sites for General Dynamics over the years that included the unions' history, membership decline, questionable financial dealings, collective bargaining records, corruption and more. Communicating to employees the rules they would have to live under in the form of the union's constitution can also be effective, and strike statistics and stories (factual, documentary-style) can be very powerful.

Develop Your Communication Plan

Now that you've gathered as much intelligence as possible, including information on the company, the union and the employees, it's time to develop a communication strategy. I know this may seem like a daunting task and you may feel that it's better to operate in a reactionary mode according to what the union might be doing, but I can assure you that if you do not develop a strategy you will have an uphill battle all the way. In order to get ahead, you need to think through your strategic plan.

That said, you must also remain flexible. Always maintain the ability to react and answer false claims, address the union's ability to rally the community, and handle tactics such as home visits and filing of ULP's. Your strategy must be modifiable to accommodate any union attacks. Continue meeting with your team on a regular basis even after the strategy is in place. Realize too that you've got a very finite period of time to work with if you've already gotten the petition.

The first step in your strategy is determining the target audience. Of course, those in the proposed or potential bargaining unit are your primary audience, but there is also a secondary (family/ spouse/community) audience that is equally important to the success of the campaign. You'll need to develop a separate plan for any audience outside your primary sphere of influence. Union tactics often include home

> *"From the beginning of January until the February election, the entire management team was fully engaged in an all-out blitz of information and communication pieces, as is typical during any company campaign. Some staff members were charged with adopting and developing the actual campaign modules and senior management at the facility would review and approve any and all materials. After each module was presented, there were numerous questions that were gathered by members of the staff through the communication teams that were established and these questions were answered in writing each and every week of the campaign. This feedback was very impressive, proved to be very effective and showed the union that we would get answers back to the employees... unlike many of the questions employees posed to union organizers."*

visits (to reach spouses and families) and community involvement with local politicians, churches and members of the clergy, newspapers, and other publicity-friendly venues. Be sure you're not neglecting an audience that the union is focusing on.

This brings us to the question of what types of communication you want to use. Decide what formats or mediums will be most effective with each target audience. Leaflets/handouts/brochures, posters, personal one-on-one meetings, group meetings, email, video, websites, and letters to the homes can all be effective vehicles when used with the right audience at the right time. In most cases, you'll need a combination of these tools.

Thinking it through, you will more than likely choose to use one or two delivery mechanisms or multiple channels. If the union is very quiet, structured team meetings typically don't work – people are afraid to talk in front of a group. In this case it is better to use the relationship the supervisor has built to connect with employees individually.

As with most things, timing is everything. Construct a deployment calendar based on the week before the petition date and working backward from there. Be sure you're reaching each employee as often as is feasible. For example, in one campaign, I began several weeks of informational sessions with supervisors on all three shifts. We then provided employees and supervisors with wage comparisons for benchmark jobs as well as benefit comparisons. This effort diffused a number of wage and benefit issues that existed due to misinformation, promulgated by the internal union organizers. Then, we began distributing a series of small different colored cards that contained questions for employees to "Ask The Organizer." This action had the desired effect of placing the internal and external organizers on the defensive.

In this particular campaign, all of the above proved to move us in the right direction. By the later part of the second month, we felt that we were at least on an even par with the union and their organizing attempts. At that point, we needed to get into a proactive mode and start working some of the issues, as well as clear up any other misconceptions that existed.

For the next two months, we continued to work on the issues with all employees and supervisors. About a month prior to when we thought the union would file a petition for election, we launched a UnionFree.com website, in which Projections provided a wealth of information about the company, wages and benefits, facts about union authorization cards, copies of all our internal and external communication pieces and a significant amount of information about

> "The management team delivered all communications with conviction and credibility. Over time, the employees learned that the Company representatives were delivering factual information and this was continued throughout the campaign."

the union. The number of hits to the site was monitored during the entire campaign and the site was also updated on a regular basis. This venture proved to cause quite a stir with the union and internal organizers and also provided another communications avenue for the company to influence our employees as well as their immediate families-that all-important secondary audience- on a 24/7 basis. For any employees who did not have personal computers at home, we provided access to computers via the computer training lab, or recommended the local library, which also offered free access.

So, you can see how providing a variety of delivery tools and communicating on a regular basis can work together to reach employees.

The final element in your communication plan should address how you want the final pre-vote message to be delivered – what's in the message, and equally important, what's not (ie: if upper management is one of the key issues, that person or people should not be a part of the final appeal). If you have a Unionfree.com website in place, use it to deliver a powerful pre-vote message. Additionally, Projections' custom-produced 25th Hour video (so-named because of the NLRB's 24-hour rule in which captive audience meetings cannot be held) can make the difference with your fencesitters, as it can truly reach employees on a different level than any other communications you may have deployed over the course of the campaign. I've used those videos in the traditional captive audience meetings as well as sending them to the homes with a personal letter to the employee and spouse or family. One new approach was making the 25th Hour Video available on the web for employees' families to view in different languages.

> "Simultaneously, a number of key employees worked with Projections, developing the custom "25th Hour" video. This video proved to have a significant impact on the remaining undecided voters. The video not only encapsulated most of the materials presented in the prior four weeks of the company's formal campaign, but also contained some damaging yet factual information about the lead union organizer."

It's truly not a matter of which communications tool to choose, but rather how the different media reaches different members of the audience. This is something I've half-jokingly called the "Publishers Clearing House" communication strategy. There are 10 or 15 different pieces of paper that fall out of that envelope, each with a different message, different approach, but they are all focused on a single outcome. So, no matter which one speaks to any particular individual, you've reached them in the most effective way possible. Choosing what will work best of course depends on your particular audiences, your business niche, the size of your business, and most importantly, your business culture. Regardless of the methods, timing is also very crucial.

A Plan In Action

The following is a very simple example of a communication plan for an active organizing drive. Your plan may be much more complex, and should address the specific issues affecting your campaign:

Immediate
*   Assemble a campaign team. The head of HR might take the lead with assistance and oversight provided by a representative from HQ.

*   Retain outside counsel to represent you at the NLRB for unit clarification hearings, ULP's, etc.

*   Begin educating the entire workforce immediately about the union's campaign to organize the business.

*   Challenge the inclusion of certain job descriptions in the union's bargaining unit definition at the NLRB, expand or shrink the unit if appropriate.

*   Get the upper hand on communications via Team Meetings with all employees and maintain this communications effort throughout the campaign.

*   Issue an internal communication reaffirming your "No harassment" policy (include your email and solicitation policy).

Near Future
*   Disseminate a card signing brochure – and also send it to the employees homes to establish spousal influence. All future communication pieces should also sent to employee's homes.

*   Show Projections' "Little Card, Big Trouble" DVD on cardsigning, also consider the video called "The Home Visit" if the union is knocking on employees' doors. Again - the family influence is very powerful.

*   Provide additional labor relations videos each week.

- Purchase through Projections, Inc. "Proud To Be Union Free" video series and "Straight Talk" videos and show these to all employees during the weekly team meetings.

- Establish a Unionfree.com website for employees and families. Capitalize on the union's absence of answers to employee questions. Answer the questions via periodic online distribution of sections of the union's Constitution. Add information to the website on dues, fees, fines, union rules and regulations.

Ongoing
- Conduct periodic straw polls to assess any progress you are making and also to determine areas to influence.

- Research and have prepared all formal campaign material, should the election actually take place. Disseminate info on Unionfree.com website. Promote employee/family use of online benefits calculator, dues calculator, and strike calculator in ongoing communication.

- Educate supervisors via Projections "Supervisors Can Keep You Union Free" training series. (This training is available on DVD and as internet-based eLearning.)

- Highlight the union's poor organizational showing and request postponements in their dealings with the NLRB (e.g. the four different petitions one union had to file just to get the proposed unit definition clarified).

- Evaluate if time is working to your advantage – are you seeing significant attrition among the internal organizers?

- Be sure the management team continues to gain confidence throughout the campaign and that they display this confidence in their positive dealings on any union organizing matter.

- Communicate about union membership statistics and include data on unionization in the private sector as well as the specific union trying to organize employees.

- Begin work on a custom "25th Hour" video. (custom video is also highly effective in the form of role plays and narrative information related to your specific issues).

Final Weeks of Campaign
- Conduct final straw polls to assess where your opportunities lie and where progress has been made.

- Provide updated campaign information on the website and in person via supervisors.

- For the two weeks prior to the vote, make significant efforts to stress the importance of having all eligible team members vote.

- Show custom "25th Hour" video in final captive audience meeting.

- Send custom "25th Hour" video to the homes with a letter from the President or post on the web. (Note: The ability to send to employees' homes depends on several variables, including the number of employees, timing, delivery method, etc.)

Where To Go From Here

Preventing future organizing campaigns begins not just with individual communication efforts, but a Multiple-Step Labor Relations Communication Strategy that is carefully constructed from beginning to end. But before the strategy can be constructed and put into place, you need to make sure there is a dedication to follow through. That may sound simple on paper, but it involves a commitment of time and money. Remember that just because you (or your department) understand the benefits of remaining union-free does not mean that upper management will be willing to dedicate the necessary budget – unless you are able to demonstrate the cost benefits of this strategy. You'll need to create your strategy and subsequently do an analysis of the cost and strategic (including competitive) benefits of remaining union-free in order to justify implementation.

> *"The above campaign efforts had the desired result - 65% voted to remain union-free. Our communication also paid off as our effort resulted in 97% of the eligible voters actually voting. This was a remarkable turnout . We communicated this event to all employees and thanked them for their patience during this long ordeal."*

This is not something that can be done overnight, and it's not something to take lightly. You need to make sure you not only have adequate staffing to accomplish the tasks you outline in your strategy, but the right people for the job. Legal support is necessary, either internally if you have those resources available to you, or externally. You'll want to learn about all the outside resources available to you, including attorneys, consultants and other companies like Projections that provide tools that will help you in your desire to remain union-free.

You need to set out by defining what it means to "union-proof" your company. That definition can include not just thwarting organizing attempts but also having the ability to answer any union efforts to publicly damage the company's reputation (known as a "Corporate Campaign"). It can mean making labor relations education for supervisors a part of their performance evaluations. It most definitely means educating employees. The following is an example of a good preventative strategy. Yours will differ as you explore all the options available to you, but this is an excellent starting point.

Step One: Start a dialogue
The first and most important step is to approach the topic of unions in an open manner. The goal here is not to make any employee feel threatened or intimidated (as that will, more often than not, backfire). What's needed initially is an introduction to the topic, what Projections calls an "Icebreaker." This fully custom video is a straightforward and frank discussion that defines who your employees are, using this as a definition to establish what it means to be an employee of your company, and why it's a point of pride. A first step into "employer branding," the custom Icebreaker sets the tone for the entire communication strategy by demonstrating that the company is not made up of the product that is delivered, the number of people employed, customers served, or countries traversed, but rather of the people, the employees. As an introduction, it will also provide the reasons why the company believes that third party intervention is not only unnecessary, but can also carry with it risks that employees may not otherwise consider.

You may also want to consider "Little Card, Big Trouble" in the early stages of employment. The NLRB approved the program for use not only in active cardsigning campaigns but also as an orientation message, and it's a powerful one. (If you'd like the full whitepaper or a transcript of the NLRB's decision on this point, please login to Projections client portal at www.ProjectionsInc.com.) This preventative discussion is most effective early, before any union gains a foothold, and in the future as new employees are hired.

Just a side note, here: I've seen companies who are afraid of the "u-word;" they think if employees hear about unions they're that much more likely to seek one out. In my experience, this is the absolute opposite of what happens. Any company afraid to talk about it becomes the unions' easiest target. If your employees aren't knowledgeable about unions, make sure you're the one to provide that information – otherwise, the union will do it for you, and not in a good way.

Step Two: Open the Door
From the moment an employee is hired, your culture of open communication must be readily apparent. One of the best things you can do is welcome new members of your team with a consistent message. I highly recommend starting out with one of Projections' comprehensive custom orientation videos. This tool has a 30 -year track record. It's proven to improve retention rates, and Projections has never seen a client that produced a custom orientation become

unionized. (More information at http://www.employeeorientations.com)

The other side of the open door is important as well. It's imperative to invite dialogue between managers and employees. Make sure managers are clear that employee concerns are important. Realizing that every manager may not be as people-oriented as you might like, a consistent forum such as a dedicated online source of labor information can be a vital resource for managers. The "Laborlook.com" website is specific to manager needs and helps managers and supervisors stay informed about labor matters in a very proactive way. Positive employee relations must be undertaken as a two-way street, and this fully custom website, centered on supervisors, provides them with the tools and resources they need to react quickly, correctly and legally, and to treat employees with respect. Combined with the Supervisors Can Keep You Union Free online training, LaborLook is an outstanding way to let managers and supervisors know they're supported. (More information at http://www.supervisors.tv and http://www.laborlook.com)

Step Three: Establish a Presence
Next, the Employee Relations, Human Resources or Labor Relations team should establish a consistent online presence for employees – one that reinforces positive employee relations by providing the information employees are seeking. A preventative version of the "Unionfree.com" custom website, which may have been used previously during a campaign can also be used in non-campaign settings. Employees must have a source that they know will provide ongoing information about the things that are important to them – one that is not just relevant, but trustworthy, timely and solid. If an organizing campaign were ever to gain a foothold, this website can be converted to a campaign-oriented communication piece, adding information about the specific union(s) targeting employees, and evolving as the issues dictate. (Additional information is available at http:// www.unionfree.com) Of course, Projections offers a variety of different URLs, such as www.employeeupdate.com, for non-campaign sites.

Step Four: Provide "Useful Information"
It's important at this point that the information the company provides is useful to employees. The question is, how do you define "useful?" You should define it as the information employees need to understand the daily workings of the company, of the support and communication channels available to them and how they are affected personally. In short, employees need to see current, relevant factual information. They need to know about the things that can affect them, and they need to know that upper management really is aware

of the challenges they face on a daily basis.

Again, a custom video is a very useful tool. Consistent communication on changes to benefits programs, healthcare costs, education on workplace issues, even environmental and economic factors that can affect the company are vital to employees' performance and loyalty. Even if you provide just an annual video update mailed to employees homes, you're taking a huge step forward to insure that employees know you understand their daily challenges and that they understand the challenges your business faces. This two-way understanding makes it far less likely employees will see a union as the solution to any of those challenges.

Online, the definition of useful information could include adding to your (employee relations focused) employee-centric website Projections' online "benefits calculator" a tool that demonstrates the true value of the benefits the company provides (and this can be created specific for each employee group if necessary), letters from management and upper management, information about unions in general, even calculators that demonstrate what they could lose if they were to go on strike. Many options exist, and the definition of "useful" may change over time, but maintaining a Unionfree.com website will provide both the company and its employees with a comforting source of current labor information.

Step Five: Maintain Ongoing Communication
I've tried to impress upon you that you cannot simply create an internal communication campaign, execute it, and walk away. Pro-active employee relations that keep companies union-free are only effective if they are ongoing. It is necessary – even required – that the company make sure that the open channels remain so. Educating and keeping supervisors informed on a regular basis is the foundation of that consistent and regular communication. (See www.LaborLook.com for a powerful and consistent way to keep managers and supervisors informed.) In your strategy, include ongoing maintenance to your supervisors' Employee Relations Training and communication. Include updates as frequently as possible (daily, weekly, monthly). Remember that in order to remain trusted sources of information, your online suggestion boxes must be answered in a timely manner, and all managers and supervisors must be well-trained and available to address employee concerns. (www.supervisors.tv highlights both video and interactive eLearning that can help you address this need.)

One final note on your overall strategy: the euphoria of winning an election passes quickly – don't rest on the year-long grace period – you must continue communicating. Remember that the union can still actively campaign; the only thing the company is protected from is having a petition filed. And one year and one day after the election, they can file a new petition. In the next chapter, we'll explore beyond the preventative strategies and examine eleven key areas to focus on best practices.

Time To Get Started

Below are eleven areas that should be examined to ensure that a business has union-free best practices in place.

HIRING/SELECTION PROCESS

- Extreme caution in the selection process must be exercised: e.g. ensure that the candidates can live with "flexible" assignments, are open-minded, won't complain if jobs or they are moved to different areas of the facility or shift ,etc.
- Good background checks most always pay dividends if there is a negative suspicion on the interviewer's part.
- Always have more than one person interview each prospective hire if at all possible.
- Know the legal "do's & don'ts" to ask.
- If you suspect a "salt," more than likely, it doesn't pay to take the risk.
- Reference checks have proven to be an unreliable exercise and the same is true in this venue – applicants seldom, if ever, provide a poor reference.

FIRST LINE SUPERVISION

- Always maintain supervisory involvement on all shifts – one can't overemphasize that the first-line team makes or breaks a union-free facility.
- First line supervision "is" the company to most employees – they are the key to affect change in this arena and a host of others.
- Establish a "core team" of specially trained union-avoidance supervisors on all shifts.
- Use this team as a sounding board for policy changes, as communication conduits, to train weaker or new supervisors.
- Front line supervision must "sell" the company's party line at all times – if they don't buy the line – it most likely won't be sold!

COMMUNICATIONS

- Communicate early, often and aggressively as practical on all matters affecting the business, human resources matters or community related items.
- Never let the rumor mill be a suitable substitute for communications.
- Never assume anyone knows anything.
- Ensure the management team takes prides in the communications efforts of the facility.
- Along with communications comes the difficult task of insuring the same team has honed their listening skills.
- Promote various communication meeting venues (e.g. breakfast meetings with facility managers, skip-level meetings, cook outs, recognition award meetings, safety meetings, service award meetings, employee-spouse benefit briefings, retirement counseling, open houses for employees and families, etc.).
- As much as possible, involve the employees' families.

UNION AVOIDANCE TRAINING

- Union avoidance training should be ongoing or at least bi-annual for all supervisors.
- Upper management should be involved, though not necessarily in every session.
- Get as sophisticated as possible with this training – the better armed supervisors are, the better they will be able to defend the facility.
- New supervisors should have a more detailed training than the seasoned professionals – they should also have a sponsor that will take them under their wings for a period of time – usually one year.

ORGANIZING (THIRD PARTY) DETECTION

- Ensure that there is a network to report any and all unusual or suspected third party activities. The LaborLook.com website is an excellent tool for keeping an eye on this sort of thing if you have multiple locations, allowing reporting of any activity in the local area as well.
- The core team of supervisors can be the conduit for such reporting and they should develop their own networks within their work areas to keep apprised of and report any activity.
- No matter how trivial the item may be, it should always be reported to the HR department or appropriate party through the website or in person.

- The reporting party should be thanked and not chastised for reporting seemingly insignificant items.
- Provide and encourage feedback from reporting sources.
- Run each and every item to the ground to detect real issues, trends and even patterns.

EMPLOYEE RELATIONS

- The representatives must walk the fine line of employee advocate and management defender.
- They should be very well versed in union avoidance/detection skills.
- They should have a presence on all shifts and "press the flesh" as much as possible. The absence of this presence will steer employees towards other representation.
- Minimize the department's perception as the "discipline administrators."
- Bring in fresh faces whenever possible to stimulate proactive thinking.

WAGE & BENEFIT STRUCTURE

- A true union-free culture should differentiate itself from unionized workers and product competitors by providing the most affordable wage and benefit structures.
- These items should be reviewed and appropriately acted upon on an annual basis, or more, if needed.
- Don't let the competition get ahead, especially if they are a union shop – this will only lead to an issue that you didn't want to have.
- Be creative in your wage and benefit structures and let the employees have input if and when appropriate – periodically do a needs analysis. Develop higher wage structures for employees who want to attain additional skills that benefit both the company and employee.

RETENTION

- Retention begins with hiring - consider a Pre-Hire Orientation video that honestly describes the company, the job and the expectations for the position.
- Crucial to any business is the retention of its workers. This is even more critical in a union-free workplace. Care must be given to provide the proper wage, benefit, and career growth to all the employees that one employs.
- When wages are maximized, be proactive and develop the employee's ability to "stretch" their skills so that additional monies can be applied when appropriate.

- Exit interviews must be a way of life. The proper analysis of these interviews as well as corrective actions can preclude unwanted attrition.
- Your onboarding of new hires should include an orientation video with the company's union-free philosophy as a part of that consistent message.

POLICIES & PROCEDURES

- Policies and procedures should always be tailored with keeping the third party at bay.
- Items like skip-level meetings, spontaneous employee recognition, general employee recognition, employee involvement, company sponsored community involvement, etc. should be developed, encouraged and fostered to the fullest extent possible.
- Every care should be taken to provide equity in these procedures for all employees.

EMPLOYEE INVOLVEMENT

- Establish teams that empower employees to provide feedback, input, and suggestions.
- These teams, when managed effectively, have proven to be a valuable extension of the management team, and can facilitate problem resolution and have an impact on the bottom line.
- Care should be given to not have these teams become an adjunct to the HR staff or be the alternative to policy development.

MANAGEMENT VISIBILITY/ACCESSIBILITY

- Management visibility on the production floor or shop areas is essential in every union-free environment. Upper management's visibility and accessibility is also a needed ingredient. Employees welcome the attention and sense that it is all part of management's commitment to the company's culture.
- The interactions must be genuine and sustained and can't be perceived as the "car salesmen" approach or the "glad-handing politician."
- The drawback in this area is the timing of the visits. Upper management should not "show" up when there is a major problem or issue. The visits should be somewhat patterned, but also somewhat spontaneous.

The long and short of this topic is that union avoidance has to be woven into the fabric of the facility (or business unit) culture. In essence, it needs to become the culture - a "cradle-to-grave" approach. If it is not lived in this light, it is conceptually broken to begin with. "Union Free" can't be what the company aspires to be - it has to be lived each and every day. Once this practice is compromised in the slightest, it presents an opening for any union to enter.

In your effort to remain union-free, the first step I'd like to recommend you take is to sign up for Projections' complimentary Insider membership. Insider members have access to full-length online previews and online ordering, as well as whitepapers, webinars, daily labor news updates, LM2's for most major unions, and much more. Beyond that, Insider Members are always the first to know of new resources as they are produced, and often receive special incentives on those new products before they are released. To sign up for free access - and receive a complimentary video, just for registering - visit the Projections website at www.ProjectionsInc.com, and click on the orange Portal link in the upper right hand corner.

Notes

Notes

Notes

Notes

CPSIA information can be obtained at www.ICGtesting.com
Printed in the USA
BVOW04s0835010415

394228BV00009B/319/P